LOOP OF JADE

LOOP OF JADE

Sarah Howe

Chatto & Windus
LONDON

3 5 7 9 10 8 6 4 2

Chatto & Windus, an imprint of Vintage,
20 Vauxhall Bridge Road,
London SW1V 2SA

Chatto & Windus is part of the Penguin Random House group of companies
whose addresses can be found at global.penguinrandomhouse.com

 Penguin
Random House
UK

Published by Chatto & Windus in 2015

www.vintage-books.co.uk

A CIP catalogue record for this book is available from the British Library

ISBN 9780701188696

Printed and bound in Great Britain by Clays Ltd, St Ives plc

Typeset by Palimpsest Book Production Ltd, Falkirk, Stirlingshire

Penguin Random House is committed to a sustainable future for
our business, our readers and our planet. This book is made from
Forest Stewardship Council® certified paper.

for my family

'These ambiguities, redundancies, and deficiencies recall those attributed by Dr Franz Kuhn to a certain Chinese encyclopedia entitled *The Celestial Emporium of Benevolent Knowledge*. On those remote pages it is written that animals are divided into: (a) belonging to the emperor, (b) embalmed, (c) tame, (d) sucking pigs, (e) sirens, (f) fabulous, (g) stray dogs, (h) included in the present classification, (i) frenzied, (j) innumerable, (k) drawn with a very fine camelhair brush, (l) others, (m) having just broken the water pitcher, (n) that from a long way off look like flies.'

— JORGE LUIS BORGES

Contents

LOOP OF JADE

LOOK CLASE

Mother's Jewellery Box

the twin lids
    of the black lacquer box
        open away –

a moonlit lake
    ghostly lotus leaves
        unfurl in tiers

silver chains
    careful *o*'s and *a*'s
        in copperplate

twisted strings
    of flattened beads
        lupin seeds

carnelians
    their tarnished settings
        horseflies' eyes

her amber ring –
    my fingers gauge
        its weight –

teaspoon of honey
    whisky poured
        by morning light

Crossing from Guangdong

Something sets us looking for a place.
For many minutes every day we lose
ourselves to somewhere else. Even without
knowing, we are between the enveloping sheets
of a childhood bed, or crossing
that bright, willow-bounded weir at dusk.
Tell me, why have I come? I caught
the first coach of the morning outside
the grand hotel in town. Wheeled my case
through the silent, still-dark streets of the English
quarter, the funereal stonework facades
with the air of Whitehall, or the Cenotaph,
but planted on earth's other side. Here
no sign of life, save for street hawkers, solicitous,
arranging their slatted crates, stacks of bamboo
steamers, battered woks, to some familiar
inward plan. I watch the sun come up
through tinted plexiglas. I try to sleep
but my eyes snag on every flitting, tubular tree,
their sword-like leaves. Blue metal placards
at the roadside, their intricate brooch-like
signs in white, which no one disobeys.
I am looking for a familiar face. There is
some symbol I am striving for. Yesterday
I sat in a cafe while it poured, drops
like warm clots colliding with the perspex
gunnel roof. To the humid strains of Frank
Sinatra, unexpectedly strange, I fingered
the single, glossy orchid – couldn't decide
if it was real. I picked at anaemic
bamboo shoots, lotus root like

the plastic nozzle of a watering can,
over-sauced – not like you would make at home.
I counted out the change in Cantonese.
Yut, ye, sam, sei. Like a baby. The numbers
are the scraps that stay with me. I hear
again your voice, firm at first, then almost
querulous, asking me not to go.
I try to imagine you as a girl –
a street of four-storey plaster buildings,
carved wooden doors, weathered, almost shrines
(like in those postcards of old Hong Kong you loved) –
you, a child in bed, the neighbours always in
and out, a terrier dog, half-finished bowls
of rice, the ivory Mah Jong tablets
clacking, like joints, swift and mechanical,
shrill cries – *ay-yah! fah!* – late into the night.
My heart is bounded by a scallop shell –
this strange pilgrimage to home.

*

The bus sinks
with a hydraulic sigh. So, we have crossed
the imaginary line. The checkpoint
is a concrete pool. The lichen-green uniformed
official, with his hat brimmed in black gloss,
his elegant white-gloved hands, his holstered
gun, slowly mounts the rubbered steps,
sways with careful elbows down the aisle. I lift
this crease-marred passport, the rubbed
gold of the lion crest – a mute offering.

Two fingers brace the pliant spine, the thumb
at the edge – an angle exact as a violinist's
wrist – fanning through stamps to halt at the last
laminated side. He lifts his eyes to read
my face. They flicker his uncertainty
as he makes out eyes, the contour of a nose:
half-recognition. These bare moments –
something like finding family.
The mild waitress in Beijing. *Your mother . . .
China . . . worker?* she asked, at last, after
many whispers spilling from the kitchen.
Or the old woman on the Datong bus,
doubtless just inviting a foreigner to dinner,
but who could have been my unknown
grandmother, for all I knew or understood.
She took a look at me and reached up
to grasp my shoulders, loosing a string
of frantic, happy syllables, in what
dialect I don't even know. She held my
awkward hands, cupped in her earthenware
palms, until the general restlessness showed
we neared the stop. As the doors lurched open,
she smiled, pressed a folded piece of paper,
blue biro, spidery signs, between my fingers,
then joined in the procession shuffling off. Some,
I realised then, were in hard hats, as they
dwindled across the empty plain, shadowed
by the blackened, soaring towers of the mine.

*

Something sets us looking for a place.
Old stories tell that if we could only
get there, all distances would be erased.
Wheels brace themselves against the ground
and we are on our way. Soon we will reach
the fragrant city. The island rising
into mist, where silver towers forest
the invisible mountain, across that small
span of cerulean sea. I have made
the crossing. The same journey you, a screaming
baby, made, a piercing note among grey,
huddled shapes, some time in nineteen-forty-
nine (or year one of the fledgling People's
State). And what has changed? The near-empty
bus says enough. And so, as we approach,
stop-start, by land, that once familiar scene –
the warm, pthalo-green, South China tide –
I can make out rising mercury
pin-tips, distinct against the blue
as the outspread primaries at the edge
of a bird's extending wing. So much
taller now than when I left
fifteen years ago. Suddenly, I know –
from the Mid-Levels flat where I grew up,
set in the bamboo grove – from the kumquat-
lined windows on the twenty-fifth floor,
tinted to bear the condensation's glare –
you can no longer see the insect cars
circling down those jungle-bordered boulevards.
The low-slung ferry, white above green,
piloting the harbour's carpet of stars,
turned always home, you can no longer see.

Start with Weather

whether they will ever return to us
    is a hard and indeterminate thing

whether the scrunched-up mind in its agony
    can parse the parakeet's tracks

whether between the powder and the peeling face
    anything actually matters

whether the dope's doubt is preferable
    to the toper's torpor

whether my pearls live with Orlando's wits
    in the moon's cold scrapyard

whether guilt's deranged orbit
    jellies the tar of parking lots

whether the Lord is my coelacanth
    who shall not weep

whether the foul-fleshed solecism
    is the queerest of fish

whether my beached pearls in their solace
    rode death's sad carousel

whether the lost will come back to us
    in an agony of parakeets

whether the courtship of crab and faux-oak finial
    will break into peeling song

(a) Belonging to the emperor

Today my name is Sorrow.
So sang the emperor's first nightingale.

The emperor was a fickle god.
He preferred to be thrilled by an automatic bird

in filigreed gold. A music box, a leitmotif.
Love me, please. Orange blossom.

I see my father bathed in the blare of that same
aria, prodding the remote

to loop. *Chiamerà, chiamerà* –
His face is red. Beneath his glasses, it is wet.

(b) Embalmed

*'The First Emperor? He buried alive 460 scholars. We have
buried 46,000!'* – CHAIRMAN MAO, 8 May 1958

West of this chamber where our breaths guttered out, nine horses
were led backward down a ramp into the pit, tethered & sealed in.
At the command, craftsmen rigged up hidden crossbows to impale

intruders. Waterways of twisting quicksilver modeled the hundred
rivers, the Yangtze & seas, contrived so they seem to flow. Above
are mapped the celestial bodies, winking in seed pearls. Man-fish

oil nourishes his lamps, calculated to burn through eras, undimmed.
In life, the First Emperor took pleasure from a hunting park stocked
with strange birds & fierce beasts offered by nations in far quarters:

the land of *K'un-ming* sent a Gold-sifting Bird as tribute. Men said
it'd hatched 9000 *li* distant, its netting an auspicious sign. This bird
is sparrow-shaped, but its colour is yellow. The Son of Heaven kept

it in the Garden for Numinous Fowl, feeding it true pearl for sweet-
meat & turtle brain for drink. It spits up powdered gold like millet,
which may be cast into utensils. In the stable pit, nine clay grooms

kneel. We didn't wait long for him: whisperers blamed the mercury
pills held up as the Elixir of Immortality; so his alchemists claimed.
Regular ingestion will induce limbs to itch & crawl with imagined

insects, the hands & feet to swell dropsically, skin to pucker & shed,
poisoning the tiny invisible demons of bodily decay &, incidentally,
the patient. A wall's thickness from those lapsed pavilions of equine

bones, excavators will find the Ghost Menagerie. Still more prized are these once-wild examples: each creature laid in its tailor-made sarcophagus, complete with jade saucer. A muntjac's spindled legs

pick amidst the Elect Herd of Spectral Deer, its nubbed skull tilted to lap from the dish. Or the pin & pumice-boned remnants of birds scooped up from their gilded perches, or snared by the forlorn crew

of zookeepers turned huntsmen so as to brighten the spiritual plane with exotic plumage & nine-tone songs. The Exalted Being expired while on a circuit of the subject states comprising his newly unified

Empire. At his death, the capital was still two months away by road. It was summer: the Supreme One's sleeping-carriage was starting to smell. We felt our own drowsy bones newly whiten & stir. The First

Minister & co-conspirators, fearing rebellion in the uncivil frontiers, contrived to mask his demise: they changed the corpse's robes daily, ordered its usual meals, & had every carriage loaded up with a *picul*

of salt-fish, for the stink. They will struggle to find a scientific term, unborn historians, for the phoenixes that roosted in his park's divine arbours. In their dreams, our long-lost books nightly buckle & char.

Earthward

I watched the shadowplay
    of trees
against the blinds
    one October –
in the way sometimes
    you stare

at a pale face across the bed
    so long
you hardly see it –
    fingers trembling,
vague as a street
    at night, as nature

stripped of accident,
    they shook
with a gusting stutter
    more restless still
for being not
    the thing itself.

(c) Tame

'*It is more profitable to raise geese than daughters.*'
— CHINESE PROVERB

This is the tale of the woodsman's daughter. Born with a box
      of ashes set beside the bed,
in case. Before the baby's first cry, he rolled her face into the cinders –
      held it. Weak from the bloom
of too-much-blood, the new mother tried to stop his hand. He dragged
      her out into the yard, flogged her
with the usual branch. If it was magic in the wood, they never
      said, but she began to change:

her scar-ridged back, beneath his lashes, toughened to a rind; it split
      and crusted into bark. Her prone
knees dug in the sandy ground and rooted, questing for water,
      as her work-grained fingers lengthened
into twigs. The tree – a lychee – he continued to curse as if it
      were his wife – its useless, meagre
fruit. Meanwhile the girl survived. Feathered in greyish ash,
      her face tucked in, a little gosling.

He called her Mei Ming: *No Name.* She never learned to speak. Her life
      maimed by her father's sorrow.
For grief is a powerful thing – even for objects never conceived.
      He should have dropped her down
the well. Then at least he could forget. Sometimes when he set
      to work, hefting up his axe
to watch the cleanness of its arc, she butted at his elbow – again,
      again – with her restive head,

till angry, he flapped her from him. But if these silent pleas had
      meaning, neither knew.
The child's only comfort came from nestling under the
      lychee tree. Its shifting branches
whistled her wordless lullabies: the lychees with their watchful eyes,
      the wild geese crossing overhead.
The fruit, the geese. They marked her seasons. She didn't long to join
      the birds, if longing implies

a will beyond the blindest instinct. Then one mid-autumn, she craned
      her neck so far to mark the geese
wheeling through the clouded hills – it kept on stretching – till
      it tapered in a beak. Her pink toes
sprouted webs and claws; her helpless arms found strength
      in wings. The goose daughter
soared to join the arrowed skein: kin linked by a single aim
      and tide, she knew their heading

and their need. They spent that year or more in flight, but where –
      across what sparkling tundral wastes –
I've not heard tell. Some say the fable ended there. But those
      who know the ways of wild geese
know too the obligation to return, to their first dwelling place. Let this
      suffice: late spring. A woodsman
snares a wild goose that spirals clean into his yard – almost like
      it knows. Gripping its sinewed neck

he presses it down into the block, cross-hewn from a lychee trunk.
      A single blow. Profit, loss.

Loop of Jade

When the television has stayed on too long, the channels ended, and all the downstairs lights switched off but one, sometimes, rarely, my mother will begin to talk, without prelude or warning, about her growing up. Then her words feel pulled up from a dark and unreflective well – willed and not willed. It isn't that this tacit contract is not tinged by our same daily fumblings, but when the men are asleep, I think she believes it's someone else's turn to listen.

Once she spoke of her horror, as a very small child, of the communal kitchen in their low-rise tenement – half-outdoors in that muggy climate, it ran across the whole row, a corridor or terrace; this space, aside from housing a blackened, static wok the size of a Western baby's bath, was also a latrine. Of squatting barefoot over the cracked tile trench and trying not to breathe. How despite themselves her eyes would follow to the nearby drain, as it sprouted – here she giggles, shivers – the glistening bodies

of cockroaches, like obscene sucked sweets. I see them, the colour of rust or shit, hitching up from the crusted grille on agile legs;

things scuttling from some dank, subterranean chamber of the head.

*

A pendant of milk-green
Jade was meant to bind
Our two young lovers.

So when Zhu was given
To another, older man,
Liang's winged heart
Stopped its fluttering.

*

Another time she tells of being made, in the bucket room, at the place she always calls a school, to wash her hair with a green detergent meant for scouring floors,

shaken from a cardboard tube. Unconscious fingers reach towards her scalp. I do not look for the candied rose-petal patches – there as long as I remember – as of mange or burns, that tell why, before leaving her room, she will so carefully layer and arrange her lovely black hair.

*

I can never know this place. Its scoop of rice in a chink-rimmed bowl, its daily thinning soup.

Harbour thunder echoes in their sleeping room: outside, the rattling, clanking bits of boats. She huddles closer to the other girls. On slight brown arms, hairs begin to lift. The brightest smack of lightning will induce (can this be right?) the bunk's iron frame, like some kind of celestial tuning fork, to zing with a preternatural hum –

a night-dead television set, its autumn storm. An inch from the wrought bar's buzzing, her child's hand trembles. I feel my own palm magnetise to hers; but something holds it back. The metal has a funny smell:

a smoking wok, or caustic soap.

*

They interred him by
The mountain road.
From the casement's
High lattice she wept:
A caged cricket. Soon
Came the wedding day
Of Zhu Yingtai, mocking

*

She tells these and other stories with a pause-pocked, melodic, strangely dated hesitancy. What I mean by this is, whenever I hear it, that halting intonation takes me back to the years when we first moved here. In those days, in her early forties, in a new country, she spoke more slowly than now, and with a subtle, near-constant nasal hum, more of a *nnnnnng* – so natural to Cantonese –

but which filled the gaps between her otherwise fluent English like the Thereminy strings in a Mandarin film score. As she chatted with the mothers of new friends, tentatively made and dropped-off to play, it seemed to me that every minute or so – I could feel it building – she would stick mid-note: raised hand stilled, chin tilted in the doorway, a wound-down marionette I willed and willed to start up its song again. A tic the local children mocked me for – that *nnnnnnnnnnng* in the playground –

as I tried not to be ashamed.

*

What could never be.
But a magic whirlwind
Stuck fast the procession

So they could not pass
Liang's wayside grave.
The draped bride, craning
Stepped from her chair –

*

Her longest and most empty pause, I've learned, comes before the word *mother*.

As in, *My – mother, she could speak Shanghainese.* This, one of her trademark non-sequiturs – at the table the family would laugh – arrived while scraping off dinnerplates several months after a trip of mine to Shanghai. It's as though she's been conducting the conversation in her head for some time and decides disconcertingly to include you. Or, one Christmas, tucking the cooled mince pies into kitchen paper: *I sometimes think she wasn't very – reliable, my –*

mother. What she told me, I don't know how much – I can believe.

In her mouth that noun worried at me. For I would never naturally use it myself – *mother* – except at an immigration office, perhaps, to total strangers, or inside the boundaries of a poem. She places it in the room's still air with a kind of resolve, and yet a sense it's not quite right – a mistranslation –

like watching her wade, one dredged step at a time, out into a wide grey strait – myself a waving spot, unseen, on the furthest shore.

*

With a clap of thunder
The tomb cracked open,
Yawned to a ravine.
And Zhu, her silk soles
Balanced a moment
On the earth's red lip,
Hurled herself in.

*

There was   a man   in a nearby district.
When I was   young and my   mother short
of money there   was a while   a lot of
times actually   when I was   sent to live
with other people.   That man was   one of
those people.   Looking back   it was better
than the   school on Macau. I learned more
at his house. There   were other children
other   girls there too.   At night
he would teach us   the old stories   all
singing together.   People   they used to
talk   about him.   These weren't just
nursery   rhymes though   I had never heard
those before either.   I mean   the classical
legends and tales.   He had a   bad
reputation.   The legends   like Shakespeare
had a lot of girls   who   dress up as boys
so they will be allowed   to go to school
or to war.   My   mother heard about it
had me   sent back to her.   When I was old
enough I had to go to the   school instead.
There was one   'The Butterfly Lovers'. It
was a poem   and also a song.   I used to
be able to sing it all. He was   kind to me.
I don't think I ever   taught you   that one.

*

Some god was watching
Our lovers' one grave –
Breathed down a breeze
Into their broken husks:
Their souls, now two
Butterflies, flicker away,
Never to be parted again.

*

It thuds into my chest, this pendent
ring of milky jade –
I wear it strung on an old watch chain –

meant for a baby's bracelet. Into its
smooth circlet
I can – just – fit a quincunx of five

fingertips. Cool on my palm it rests –
the sinople eye
on a butterfly's wing. When I was born

she took it across to Wong Tai Sin,
my mother's mother,
to have it blessed. I saw that place –

its joss-stick incensed mist, the fortune-
casting herd,
their fluttering, tree-tied pleas – only later

as a tourist. As for the jade, I never wore
or even saw it
then. The logic runs like this: if baby

falls, the loop of stone – a sacrifice –
will shatter
in her place. Painfully knelt on the altar

step, did the old woman shake out a sheath
of red-tipped
sticks, and pick one, to entreat my fate?

And if I break it now – will I be saved?

rain, *n.*

1.*a.* The scent of hyacinths
over bus lanes.

b. From rust-tipped
scaffolding ascend the faery towers
of St Pancras, wet tannoy imploding
King's Lynn 7.45, as the black
ghost of a pigeon crests a white-
washed window.

Night in Arizona

The last of the sheet I shuffle off an ankle –
a sound like the spilling of sand
from shovel and the night air blurs

for a second with its footfall.
Our entwined shape a word in the dark.
On my forehead and cheek

each flourishing
charge of your breathing
is a moment's reprieve. Heat

in this place goes deeper than sleep,
wraps everything, increases sheen –
the forearm weighing your flank

as, dreaming, you turn from me,
curlicues slick on the backs
of thighs, my hand at your neck

and eyes aware of several kinds of dark
struggling to perfect themselves
– the hidden chair, the bouquet of our clothes

the razory arms of a juniper rattling crazily
at the edge of that endless reddening haze –
glad we move on to the city at dawn.

(d) Sucking pigs

Between choosing canapés and favours I read
how the groom's family by Chinese tradition
should gift to her kinsmen a piglet, milk-fed,
just a moon at the teat, crisped to perfection,

when quite satisfied the bride's still intact.
I imagine your mother cranking the spit.
Crackling's coy, brittle russet then succulent fat –
that atavistic aroma makes me salivate,

you physically sick. So as pet names go, *Shikse*'s
not a bad fit. (I did play your Circean temptress...)
Wikipedia says it comes down from Leviticus,
how your God labelled creatures unclean to ingest;

but then, disgust seems to blur into reverence.*
*Cf. Xu Bing, *A Case Study of Transference*

Chinoiserie

I said *Sleepy Willow*. You said *Voiture*.

That was one of our shorter arguments.
My hands twist inside your sprung hands

till we feel the lack of the smallest human

mittens trapped inside them – squirming rose,
a nest of looping ratlets – such petulant joy.

Imagine a dustless mantelpiece in what we'll call

the past. There rests a tiny, puzzling globe –
feel its chisel-riddled crust – like the most precious

of golfballs, forgot on its rosewood tee. Look,

it's actually twelve concentric ivory spheres which
all spin freely, whittled by unimaginable hands

from one elephant-smelling hunk: a machine for doing

nothing; a dragon's pearl that's rolled away. Frailest
of armillaries, whose star-dinted, independent heavens

turn on the innermost yellowing pea – one that stands

for this misbegot earth. Some nights you comfort
me with sterile knuckles, your nibbled nailbeds

ragged as the ghost of a motheaten tux. You

remind me of our lost chimneysweep and
sometimes it's too much – nose like a leaky

spigot, moppy brow. Those long-necked gestures.

You sing to me of machinists – how even in sleep they
sentry a watchmaker lathe, imagining themselves

in strobe-lit celestial factories, holding an ink-bloom pupil

to the closing eye of a vernier scale, balancing
an atom in the aptest calliper. Anxious wives watch

their somnolent hands, turning tools to invisible wheels.

(e) Sirens

pickerel, n. 1 – *A young pike; several smaller kinds of N. American pike*
pickerel, n. 2 – *A small wading bird, esp. the dunlin,* Calidris alpina

I see it clearly, as though I'd known it myself,
     the *quick look* of Jane in the poem by Roethke –
that delicate elegy, for a student of his thrown
     from a horse. My favourite line was always *her*
sidelong pickerel smile. It flashes across her face
     and my mind's current, that smile, as bright and fast
and shy as the silvery juvenile fish – glimpsed,
     it vanishes, quick into murk and swaying weeds –
a kink of green and bubbles all that's left behind.

I was sure of this – the dead girl's vividness –
     her smile unseated, as by a stumbling stride –
till one rainy Cambridge evening, my umbrella
     bucking, I headed toward Magdalene to meet an
old friend. We ducked under The Pickerel's
     painted sign, its coiled fish tilting; over a drink
our talk fell to Roethke, his pickerel smile, and
     I had one of those blurrings – glitch, then focus –
like at a put-off optician's trip, when you realise

how long you've been seeing things wrongly.
     I'd never noticed: in every stanza, even the first,
Jane is a bird: wren or sparrow, *skittery pigeon.*
     The wrong kind of pickerel! In my head, her
smile abruptly evolved: now the stretched beak
     of a wading bird – a stint or purre – swung
into profile. I saw anew the diffident stilts
     of the girl, her casting head, her gangly almost
grace, puttering away across a tarnished mirror

of estuary mud. In Homer, the Sirens are winged
    creatures: the Muses clipped them for their failure.
By the Renaissance, their feathers have switched
    for a mermaid's scaly tail. In the emblem by Alciato
(printed Padua, 1618) the woodcut pictures a pair
    of chicken-footed maids, promising mantric truths
to a Ulysses slack at his mast. But the *subscriptio*
    denounces women, *contra naturam,* plied with hind-
parts of fish: *for lust brings with it many monsters.*

Or take how Horace begins the *Ars Poetica,*
    ticking off poets who dare too much: mating savage
with tame, or snakes with birds, can only create such
    horrors, he says, as a comely waist that winds up
in a black and hideous fish. The pickerel-girl swims
    through my mind's eye's flummery like a game
of perspectives, a corrugated picture: fish one way
    fowl the other. Could it be that Roethke meant
the word's strange doubleness? *Neither father*

nor lover. A tutor watches a girl click-to the door
    of his study with reverent care one winter evening –
and understands Horace on reining in fantasy.

(f) Fabulous

Chimera, chimera –

    where does your garden grow?
A grafted Paradise. A mouthful of snow.

A Trojan conception – maculate cargo.
A spliced mouse – its unearthly day-glo.

Pythagoras's Curtain

Nightly trapped in the nearly
invisible sweet hibiscus,
cicadas somehow never seen

cadenza the acousmatic dusk.
Concealed strings, their chitinous
glissandi, stir up every treeless

gap. Iambs crisped, adrift from source –
the chanting of a lost Pythagoras.
Behind a curtain's lamp-cast shade,

he would ravel out his doctrines
while the bunched students strained
to catch the drone of that Ionian

Oz, revealing things beyond their eyes:
how numbers hum, and the planets
are tuned to a blacksmith's blows

in unheard chords; how our spirits
will wrench free at the root, and yet
those restless souls must flit from thief,

to philosopher, to plangent cricket;
how he himself recalled four lives
and one night heard a dead friend

cry from the throat of a Molossian
hound. They sing to the living. Listen:
each heartsick cicada shrilling on.

(g) Stray dogs

'Thou art a beaten dog beneath the hail'
— EZRA POUND, Canto LXXXI

To think again of Pound, bared to the sky at Pisa.
The traitor's cage they built for him specially. 6 x 6 ft
of airstrip mesh & dust. Wire diamonds shadowed
starkly underfoot. Day 25, DTC doctors transfer him
to a medical tent (*A swollen magpie in the fitful sun*)
fearing the first signs of a breakdown. Three weeks i'
this here sun goan change a man, thinks Mr Edwards
(he with the face *of the Baluba mask*) as he flips over a
packing crate, hang reg'lations, to fashion the traitor
a writing table. Squat at his crate-cum-desk, Pound
spreads flat the worn-out covers of his dog-eared
Confucius: he'd slipped it in his slacks' side pocket
that day at the house, a rifle butt pounding the door.
As he flicks through the *Analects*, his hand starts to
tremble. He pushes it hard into his temple. Takes up the
donated pencil stub: *Pull down thy vanity*. Near
illegible. Scrawling on squares of shiny latrine roll
now lodged in a library's vaults. Later he gets hold
of a G.I. pad, ruled lines turned ninety-degrees
like bars. No longer blithely ranting on Rothschilds
as in his radio days (*Whether they are born Jews,
or have taken to Jewry*). Circe's sty. Glorious cant.
Our captive flutters again to the much-thumbed page
where, having lost his disciples at the city's east gate,
Kung takes with equanimity the stranger's slur:
'Look at this man here, he has a face like a lost dog!'
'Yes,' smiles Kung Fu-tzu, 'yes, that's quite correct.'

(h) The present classification

Being herself a grotesque, perhaps the Sphinx had some
feeling for the man who was both victor and victim – did a tear
trickle down from cheek, to breast, to paw? *What creature
goes on four legs, two legs, and finally three?* Such celestial
ironies have their humbler enquirer in the Sunday-school child
who almost puts up – but doesn't quite – his pre-pubescent hand
to ask the ageing Sister about mankind's expanding family tree
one generation from Adam and Eve. This same uneasy story
being the funded subject of some Doctor of Paleoanthropology,
more used to fingering arrowed flints in lint-free cotton gloves
than pondering the stained alleles, shuffled and stacked
by the exoduses of early hominids. She doesn't know it, but she's
haunted by those 'small family pockets' of not-yet-people, trapped
a desert's span from extinction; by whether the blackened skull
she's nicknamed *Miranda*, unearthed in a dusty cave-site grave
and interspersed with the numbered fingerbones of her son –
her probable lover – and the fragmented fibula of a daughter /
granddaughter, felt anything like the shame their researcher
betrays in the euphemism of her title: *Stone Age Migrations
and the Problem of Exogamy*. Think how Antigone,
in the play that really belongs to her father, is revealed to live
in a riddle of genealogy. Or her unlikely latterday incarnation
in the plot of Polanski's grainy, neo-noir LA: Faye Dunaway's
fur-draped, ill-fated femme, when confronted by the raging
private detective who is Jack Nicholson and who loves her
takes each of his slaps – her cheek, then her other cheek,
then the first, and again, and again – until she can barely speak those
two words that sound at first like polarities, until we realise,
terribly, with him, the special violence done to her, and to language's
taxonomies – that it is possible, though we have no word,
to be someone's sister and mother. Cursed offspring of a riddled,
blinded Theban king, left to die in the desert, between human and beast.

To all Laments and Purposes

Against platinum birches
     I want nothing here – but you.

We have trees at home. Shall I
     wing you the courtyard fountain's

midnight palaver, to lull
     the list of your lonely sleep?

Love is wicker, then water;
     marriage an avenue of

limes, but not the bitter kind.
     I'm stood at the north extreme:

the reflecting pool unrolls
     a shadow world of clouds &

yews, another far orchard,
     enamelled pavilions.

It's shaking hardly at all.
     My nights are aloner too.

(i) Frenzied

Maybe holding back
is just another kind

of need. I am a blue
plum in the half-light.

You are a tiger who
eats his own paws.

The day we married
all the trees trembled

as if they were mad –
be kind to me, you said.

MONOPOLY (*after Ashbery*)

I keep everything until the moment it's needed.
I am the glint in your bank manager's eye.
I never eat cake in case of global meltdown.
I am my own consolation.

I have a troubled relationship with material things:
I drop my coppers smugly in the river.
(I do everything with an unbearable smugness.)
I propose a vote of thanks.

I make small errors in your favour. Sometimes
I pretend nothing is wrong.
I won second prize in a beauty contest.
I am yellowing at the edges.

I was last seen drawing the short straw.
I hang about tragically on street corners, where
I hand out cards that read: *if you see*
I am struggling to lift this card, please, do not help me.

(j) Innumerable

Poem on the eve of May 35th

In the early summer of 1989, when I was five, my parents took me on an unusual outing. It wasn't that the Jockey Club's Happy Valley track (at that time still epitheted 'Royal') was unfamiliar to me: every week I went there for an hour's swimming lesson in the too-hot pool, my reward an orange ice lolly from the freezer cabinet behind the clubhouse bar. But I knew things were different that morning. For one, I had never trod on the actual grass before. On race days, that was the preserve of the slow processing row of black-trousered labourers, their cone hats and canes, who would follow on after the rumbling of the horses – their job, with a practised touch as of the blind, to feel out the slightest hoof-flung sod and tamp it back into the reperfected turf. I spent the day hoisted on my father's shoulders, staring out across the jellied mass of human heads. On the big screen, the dots of light weren't tickering the customary shifting dance of odds, but the exact words that would rise from the rippling mouths in the stands' atoll, as the crest of skyscrapers stood watch. On the news that evening I tried to pick out my waving self among the banners' swell, the toy-box people chanting and abuzz. A few days later there were different pictures on the news. A man with two white shopping bags edging crabwise on a faceless boulevard in another city where twenty three years later I would struggle for over half an hour to hail a cab. On rainy race days the turf workers, still bamboo-brimmed, would wear transparent macs dotted with drizzle and the determination of a search party. Where they pressed the clumps back down, you would never know.

A Painting

I watched the turquoise pastel
melt between your fingerpads;
how later you flayed

the waxen surface back
to the sunflower patch
of a forethought, your

instrument an upturned
brush, flaked to the grain –
the fusty sugar paper buckled.

You upended everything,
always careless of things:
finest sables splayed

under their own weight,
weeks forgotten – to emerge
gunged, from the silted

floor of a chemical jamjar.
I tidied, like a verger
or prefect, purging

with the stream from the oil-
fingered tap. Stop,
you said, printing

my elbow with a rusty index,
pointing past an ancient
meal's craquelured dish

to the oyster-crust
at the edge of an unscraped palette –
chewy rainbow, blistered jewels.

Life Room

Turpentine sky unfurls through steeples and slates; the warehouse
eyes of Shoreditch blink in turn –
far off the trickling cars, the bright red bus that weaves its way to
Spitalfields, Hoxton, Bethnal
Green with purposeful inconsequence. In the darkening corner by
the sink Apollo half-springs
from his sandals, outspreading his pleat-slung marble arm. Day's
last glints snatch their chance,
blinding from behind the crawl of a monolithic cloud, to stripe the
dim floor with violent
diagonals of treacle light. The easels tilt their flatness to the sky, as
if to chase the sun – she is not
beautiful, this girl. She pads around the box, undoes the heavy flannel
gown (hangs like a man's); hesitates
before sloughing it quickly from her shoulders and crumpling its folds
with conspicuous, ritual care.
Hoisting back into the pose, her ankle involuntarily twitching, she
shuffles herself over blue
nylon drapes and, an upturned beetle, struggles to fit her forearms
to the hastily chalked guides.
Her plait has fallen differently on the pillow. I can now see the third
joint of her little finger resting
between her breasts. Again charcoal's querulous hymn, quickening
against October light. The bald man
to my left draws like an architect. What a waste of this guttering day!
Remember: pose sinks in time.
The concave stomach's hazy diminuendo; the elbow's nick. The
masking tape wafts and my miniature
world crazes to the right. I can taste charcoal on my lip. And I think
of the time when I'll only feel this
in memory, this stark, unsought, implacable stab of love

for the ugly girl's peculiarly graceful fingers, as their hanging tips curl
almost to her tilted mouth.
I'll see them one day as I open a book, or make the bed, or rush down
the road from the tube in the morning.

(k) Drawn with a very fine camelhair brush

Late spring. A scholar sits in his study.
After much contemplation
he lends his brush the ideal pressure –
leaves his mind there, on the paper.

*

Landing at Canton, the first Jesuits believed
they'd stumbled on the lost language of Eden –
that Ham had helped offload the Ark
then set off for the East, its walled lands,
taking with him Adam's perfect tongue
that named the animals one by one.
As the hopeful missionaries learned to see
in that strangely branching pagan script
the fletched fir of *tree*, the strung
crescent of *moon* – they found God's awe
in each fabulous character – each one
a nest of lacquer boxes
worlds within worlds
where meaning was a garden
where you could wander forever
in the scent of peach blossom, following the river.

木
月

*

A hand, a brush, its inclination –
involved in an anchoring of sign to thing
so artful that we, like the Jesuits, might forget

words' tenuous moorings

*

Picture a journeying scholar-poet, headed downriver –
let's say to visit a distant friend – when he's caught
by a still and peaceful spot, where the petals'
languid drift across the blue-brown mirror
is the only sign, in this pool-like lull, of the water's
relentless drive. He might lodge his little boat
under a peach tree's bough and, choosing a flattish
patch of bank, fold his long robe under his knees
to admire, overhead, the slant of a black branch
still damp from a shower – its cursive script
ghosting across the stream's spread scroll.
There, in the gently buzzing shade, he meditates
on the restless dragonflies –
the large green kind, and the smaller red,
which hover above their blurred other-selves
then dart elsewhere, to hang once more,
their slender silvered wings – too quick to see –
a marriage of stillness and furious motion.

*

This last scene being our mistranslation –
since what he sees is not the fierce miniature
offspring of a fly and dragon's astonishing tryst,
but a word, like two jewelled eyes, of mirrored   蜻蜓
worlds. He learned them as a child: each tapering
stroke of *snake-thin insect*; how the camelhair tip
traces through *green*, tangles up *go* and *stop*.
This last gesture – a sketch of a man at rest –
also happening to hold the word for *scholar*.

40

*

Our scholar reclines, as the sun burns out
over shaded water; greets the moon
with a flask of clear, sweet wine –
drinks her health – and falls asleep
reflecting how he must write a poem
about the *dragonflies*, their perfect
ligature of colour and motion – to wake
hours later, cheek wet with morning,
to discover his badly knotted skiff

has disappeared downstream

Banderole

diminutive of Fr. *bannière*
used in war of a lance's
streaming flag; in art,
the resourceful painter's
only means to make
mute canvas speak –
whereby a tawny scroll's
unfurling coil will stretch
self-involutedly away from
a boot-faced shepherd's
startled lips exhaling
their small consternation
at deity – a breath that lifts
beribboned & scripted
in the age's neat Blackletter
to signify the silent noise
– a Latinity beyond
his own lacked letters –
of the frozen man's half-joy
half-penance – its skyward
path a virgin's curl
or trumpeting pennant –
up, and further up, into
how a Northern master saw
the scumbled heavens
one midwinter

Woman in the Garden

after Bonnard

What you see on entering a room –
        the red-checked
        blouse, burning
on a chairframe in the attic crook,
        will last a lifetime.
She smiles to see her slim form continue
        in the sunlit legs
of the stool, the lilac towel fallen across its face,
        and she thinks –
wisteria peeling from the house one mid-April –
        head cocked
as if marooned on the way to a word.

        Mustard flashes
wildly up the wall: the mirror
        is a locked garden
and sometimes she visits that country.
        Through its keyhole
        the stool in miniature
wades a cobalt sea, or some accurate idea of sea –
        a greybird
        with salmon feet
engaged in telling things new
        a song veined
with rust from the throat.

She wants someone who will teach her the names
        of trees
their alien natures: the mimosa's trembling
        yellow and the ornate

mainmast of the ash. The only thing she ever
            longed for
was an enamel bath, the running water
            tinged
with cochineal, a window, somewhere
            heightening the tone –
            the bay at Cannes,
the mountains of the Estérel.

Death of Orpheus

after Streckfus

& since they move as a grove, the young ones, the walking ones, we
regard them as almost kin of our forest

& they shake with alternate winds, for their swaying follows an invisible sun

& we hear from the olives of Cithæron how these – yes, *women* –
grow in prolific contortions

& blow in the god's good wake to leave only pounded dust

& split fruit

& they tear at those strange, sloughable petals

& those of their fellows, till their pleached boles shine with the
suppleness of springtime

& their throats wail the wrenching of boughs, rooted terror, half-
sensed fires

& at last they discover their reluctant observer; this a different *genus*

& the charcoal of his singular grief, it moves us – a still thing, a slow
thing, in the now's ever-flickering

& our high heads bow in time with the flensed lyre, wood of our wood

& too swift for our perceiving, they set to stripping his branches, husk
from seed

& a lone kernel floats down the Hebrus, in search of yielding shores

(l) Others

*'I will multiply your descendants as the stars of the heaven, and
as the sand which is upon the seashore'* – GENESIS, 22:17

I think about the meaning of *blood*, which is (simply) a metaphor
and *race*, which has been a terrible pun.

*

From *castus* to *chaste*, with a detour for *caste*.
English, 廣東話, *Français d'Egypte*, מאַמע־לשון: our future children's skeins,
carded.

*

A personal Babel: a muddle. A Mendel?
Some words die out while others survive. *Crossbreed. Half-caste. Quadroon.*

*

Spun thread of a sentence: . . . *have been, and are being, evolved.*
The spiralling path from Γένεσις to *genetics*. Language revolves like a ream
of stars.

*

A different generation: *They wouldn't escape by the Mischlinge Laws.*
I wonder if they'll have your blue eyes.

*

My Carol Service reading on the seed of Abraham: tittering.
The *sand which is upon the seashore* had made them think of a picnic lunch.

46

Crocodile

Over the years they had had many similar meals. The starter was a chilled pea soup, its oddity just enough to hold the attention; that unexpected cold, spreading in waves over teeth and tongue. At that moment, the blunt end of his spoon connected softly with the table. The evening light skewed down from the high-up windows and glittered off a hundred knives poised to cut. Maybe she was thinking how quickly the summer would go from now on. He feared that she would leave him and said so too often when they were alone. She looked down at her napkin, then up; in that second, when no eyes met, it seemed perfectly right that words should be things you have to digest. Why had she had to say it? He imagined all the conversations in the room pouring from their unknown protagonists as though from the excised stomach of a hulking and battle-scarred crocodile, an eighteen-footer dragged straight from the Cretaceous. When the triumphant fisherman tipped up that membranous sac, out would gush an uncontrollable bilge of fluorescent green goo: he watched it swilling across the restaurant's parquet, chuckled as the tray-poised waiters skidded on their windmilling hams, so many Michael Flatleys. As the reeking ooze receded, the diners became aware of diverse objects beached between their corroded chair legs: asymmetrically polished stones, the barb-stripped calami of ibis or other broad-quilled waders, one rifled musket's intact silver flintlock, a small girl's hand, an acid-dinted comb.

(m) Having just broken the water pitcher

> 'Baizhang picked up a water pitcher, set it on a rock, and posed this question: "If you cannot call it a water pitcher, what do you call it?"' – WUMEN HUIKAI, *The Gateless Gate*

This fact I can't forget: my thirtieth year
had hastened by before I learned to see
how *plum blossom* lies one sidelong stroke   梅

of gum-suspended soot away from *regret*.   悔
It's said the man who invented writing,
charged with this burden by the emperor,

sought inspiration in the surface moods
of water; that he was by the river
when he spied in the finely cracking mud

a hoofprint, its brim still as a bronzed mirror,
stamped there by some invisible creature –
and understood his task. The moment he sketched

the first character, the sky rained millet
and the ghosts wailed all night for they could not
change their shapes. Five thousand years later

in some remote coal-mining district
sits an anonymous blogger, his face lit
by more than just the ancient monitor.

He ponders how strange it is (how useful . . .)
that *I beg you for the truth* is pronounced
the same as *I beg you, Elephant of Truth!*

Or that *sensitive words* (as in filters,
crackdowns) sounds exactly like *breakable
porcelain*. Done typing, he clicks *Submit*.

Recall the old monk's koan, the correct
reply to Master Baizhang's question:
His pupil kicked over the pitcher and left.

The Countess of Pembroke's Arcadia

(*P.S. 1554–1586*)

Yesternight the candle
                              scarcely
            struck
& yet its fizzled premonition held
            (sweet captive)
to a warped page that will never love ink.

Beware Zutphen
                        & the penman's matachin
            suddenly undone:
all gored thigh and selflessness.

Reading is
                        a reaching
a sister's grief; handspans
groped across the dark.

veni, veni –

Dying is such thirsty work.

(n) That from a long way off look like flies

More a midge really, flower-pressed: pent
in this hinged spread of my undergrad
Shakespeare. Down the page, a grey smudge
tinged with a rusty penumbra, like blood –
mine or its? Two sheer wings, stilled mid-word,
trace out a glyph in a strange alphabet.

At empathy's darkening pane we see
our own reflected face: *how, if that fly
had a father and mother?* On the heath, Lear
assumes all ragged madmen share
ungrateful daughters. The way my father,
in his affable moods, always thinks you
want a gin and tonic too. I wonder
if I should scrape her off with a tissue.

[There were barnacles . . .]

'Once there were . . .' – CORMAC MCCARTHY

There were barnacles that marked the edges of oceans. Late scramblers on the rocks could feel their calcic ridges stoving sharply underfoot. The wet rocks glittered beneath and in the wind they smelled of verdigris. The barnacles fused in intricate settlements. For their whole lives they cleaved, and in turn the fragile rock cleaved to them. Volcanoes and thimbles and strange constellations. Together they mapped distant cities and willed the sea to overtake them. And when the russet tide came they opened themselves like unfamiliar lovers. The whole thing some actinic principle: a forest grew up in a second, to grace a world where the sun was a watery lamp. Where none had been before, white mouths frilled softly in the current and squat armour issued forth the unlikeliest of cilia: transparent, lightly haired, cherishing each updraft as, feathered, they moved with it. They only existed for that half-sunk terrain. And as they briefly lived, those tender quills wrote of their mystery.

Faults Escaped

I wake to a sodium forest. Passengers
    speed through tickering afterglows.
    The bright underpass thirsts tonight.

In shuttered factories machines hum on
    and daylight shakes itself out. Imagine
    mounting over the corrugated world,

imagine how it arrows: one upside down
    eye after another, snatches of heaven
    in a misted spoon. Then they are gone.

I like to listen for the gabble of surfaces –
    all summer the dripping walls, the wind-
    blown gate unable to stop. They say

belief is a comfort. Still, the whispering
    as the ants dismantle every flaw, insert
    themselves in cracks like keys, all summer,

and how the wet grout crumbles tonight
    into honey and all my pretty tiles lie slumped.
    The shopfront trembles in its shutters.

Night is a veiled and silent mother;
    a living cave, the stirrings in the sides,
    water pushing blindly through a stone –

each cold diamond determined to be born.
    Too soon they leave, their love a bloom
    of salt; those encaustic tears, the stars.

The Walled Garden

Across the road, the girls quit school in threes
and fours, tripping off at speed to stations

or familiar cars, their silhouettes, slung
with shoulder bags and hockey sticks, like mules.

Remember, says the afternoon; the shut
door shudders brassily beneath my hand.

It is already dark, or darkening –
that sky above the dimming terraced rows

goes far beyond a child's imagining.
I tread along the backstreet where the cabs

cut through behind the luminous science labs –
their sills of spider plants in yoghurt pots

among the outsize glassware cylinders
like pygmies contemplating monoliths.

You cannot walk the other side because
the walled garden meets the road direct

in pools of spangled tarmac after rain;
the open gutter choking up with leaves.

As though to listen, the colossal trees
lean out into the tungsten-haloed street.

I meet another on the road – this snail's
slow ribbon turns the asphalt into gold.

Islands

At the boarding school we used to chant them
Ping Chau, Cheung Chau, Lantau, Lamma . . .
I rolled their sounds around my mouth
till they were strange again, like savouring
those New Year candies – small translucent moons
waning on the tongue. Wrapped in packages
from home that never came. This was called
'geography', for knowing where we are and names
of fixed and distant things. The words came back to me
like dreams – sometimes only that insistent rhythm –
the rocking of the rope-prowed ferry, every minute
further from Macau, that isle of lotuses, my feet
slipping on the wet, wood deck, stretching up to feel
the terseness in the air, to catch the islands
swim like mist on the horizon. Passing fish huts perched
like spindly seabirds, foaming lacework
whispering into nothing on the rocks.
My heart was drowning – the long anticipated sight
of home. In the early years, we slept
three small girls to each shelf of the beds
like dumplings stacked in steamers, someone said.
Each night lifting the stout, sculpted planks
one at a time off the iron bedframe, knuckles tight.
Without a word, we let each end thud
heavy on the ground as though pounding
red beans into paste. The lice went running.
We squashed them with our sandaled feet but many
got away. We lay beneath that charcoal blanket
too heavy for the torpid summers; colour
of the August harbour in the rains.
We lay together breathing in that odour.
Sea-drizzle. Diesel. Damp, black hair.

In October, typhoon season dwindles:
washed-out stars suspended in the puddles
where our faces floated by, white bellies of dead fish.
That year, before Mid-Autumn came we learned
to write 月. Haltingly, I penned the crescent
strokes of combinations from the board. It seemed
a ladder to the heavens, leading up and off
the yellowed page. The faded grid of squares grew
fainter. The desk beneath my hand was pocked
and battered like the surface of the moon. That
afternoon was following *Chang'e*. Her story.
One day, through curiosity, she swallowed down
a bright pill hidden in a box – *Houyi's* Elixir of
Immortality. As he watched in horror, she floated
off into the thinning blue. Her long sleeves trailed
like cloud around a mountaintop, the moon
at first a pill, and then a swelling pearl, in the dark
mouth of the sky. He couldn't bear to shoot her
down with his star-felling bow. She lives there, cold
and lonely now. You can see her if you look.

*

I often did. Waiting for the shadowed moon to rise
into the windowframe, a pale, dependable friend.
It took my mother many months to eat the gifts
of mooncakes; four cloud-encrusted islands drifting
in their silver tin. She would take a slice
each afternoon with cups of wine, the kind we
heated in a beaten kitchen pan. An autumn treat
accompanied by cooling evenings, too rich
for more habitual food. She cut into the patterned

casing. Full moon, half moon, quarter moon.
I loved the unexpected orb inside: a golden
yolk set in a firmament of lotus paste. They glowed
like all those tiny suns trapped in lanterns
at the festival, speared on slim red candles.
Their charring wicks were cedars twisted in the wind.
I had a paper globe. Its redness smouldered
like a burnt-out star. Other children had the shapes
of animals, crimson cellophane on wired frames –
the undulating waves of dragons, sharp-beaked
cranes, all in profile like the oval forms of fish.
In the blackness of Victoria Park their skin
was gleaming gelatine, the hatching chrysalides
of ghostly moths; a single, silver sequin
marked each winking, convex eye. The ruby
stain of lamplight over water. Fishlines trailed
from them, metallic ribbons – some fluttered off
like slanting rain to settle in the shrivelled grass.
The procession trod them in the moonlit dust.

*

The first thing I remember is the sickly
pungency of camphor. My mother hired me
a bedspace in the thin-partitioned tenement
we shared with other families, one of many.
It was summer. Sweltering in the box-space of her
plastered room, its single grime-barred window, heat
poured over us in humid troughs like the bilge
of a tropical sea. She lay on the floor, stiffly,
in the keel-shadow of the bed. I fanned her,
cross-legged, from the doorway. There was no other place.
The elastic in my underwear had gone. The swishing
fan was mouthing something in the dark; its silent arc

the wafting arms of underwater weeds. Her shiny face
was deep into the light-poured, drowning world
of sleep. I was four perhaps, or three. Small enough
to fit into the open wooden storage-chest
out in the hallway, freighted with that resinous
scent of aromatic lumber clinging to the moth-
proofed, folded winter clothes of the family
who held the let. It made a child-sized bed.
My dreams were diving through the fish-eye
glow of four electric candle-bulbs; their redness
hesitating on the finely spiralled filaments
the sidelights of a far-off ship. Or the microscopic
coal-flecks of the barely smoking joss sticks, sweet
to pacify the spirit tenants of their ancestral shrine.
The crinkled polaroids half-settled in the sand.
Their hungering voices; I slept inside my treasure chest.
Baby Moses flowing through the watermeadows.
She was always taking in abandoned things.
I think she saw her sadnesses reflected in them.
Once it was a stray puppy. She gave him to me.
But the next day, fawning, absently, gifted him
to strangers. Some years later, in her violent anger
I learned it was the same with me –
a Guangdong cobbler's foundling daughter. She
said she saved me from the refuse heap, from
being eaten by the dogs with other scraps.
Too many mouths to feed. I never wondered
about these unknown siblings. Or my father's
blackened hands, turning the warm hide
of a fraying shoe beneath his hammer.
Or my real mother. Unreachable across
the water, as planets circling in the night.

Yangtze

The moon glimmers
in the brown channel.
Strands of mist
wrap the mountainsides
crowded with firs.

Declining cliffs
sink beneath vast water.
By remote paths,
twisting pines.

Far downstream
two sides
of a half-built bridge
fail to meet.
Our crude boat
chugging
points to Chongqing.
As someone I now forget
once said
journeying is hard.

My face greets
the evening breeze
I listen –
the dream of a place.

A cormorant dives
by trembling light.
From the white
eyelet of a star
the sound of ripples.

*

A fisherman
skirting shore
in his high-prowed skiff
crossing bamboo oars
comes up with a jolt –
nets catch not fish
but the wizened finger
of a submerged branch
for below
a sunken valley persists –

slick bare trunks
furred in wafting fronds
have water for sky,
ghost forest.
Roots rot deep in the hill
where buried rock
is still dry.

Windows film,
doors drift open
in the empty concrete
shells of houses
towns that once
held hundreds
of thousands
slowly filling with
what, what is it
they fill with?

Someone I now forget
once said
journeying is hard.
The moon glimmers
in the brown channel.

Notes

The epigraph is taken from *The Analytical Language of John Wilkins* by Jorge Luis Borges; the translation, with minor alterations, is the one that appears in Michel Foucault, *The Order of Things*.

BELONGING TO THE EMPEROR: *Chiamerà, chiamerà* – 'He will call, he will call'. From '*Un bel dì vedremo*' in Puccini's *Madama Butterfly*.

EMBALMED: The events known as the 'burning of books and burying of scholars' took place during the reign of *Qin Shi Huangdi*, first emperor of China, between 213 and 210BC. This poem borrows from *Sima Qian*'s *Records of the Grand Historian: Qin Dynasty*, and E.H. Schafer's 'Hunting Parks and Animal Enclosures in Ancient China' (*Journal of the Economic and Social History of the Orient* 11).

TAME: According to old Chinese custom, the midwife placed near the birthing bed a box of ashes scraped from the hearth so that, if female, the baby might be easily smothered.

FABULOUS: 'GFP is a protein derived from the jellyfish *Aequorea victoria*, which emits green light upon illumination with blue light' (Hofker and van Deursen, *Transgenic Mouse: Methods and Protocols*).

STRAY DOGS: Italicised phrases come from Ezra Pound, *The Pisan Cantos*, and '*Ezra Pound Speaking*': *Radio Speeches of World War II*.

INNUMERABLE: In Chinese, the Tiananmen incident of 1989 is known by its date – June 4th – references to which are censored on the mainland. For a time, the invented date 'May 35th' allowed Chinese web users to circumvent the ban.

OTHERS: 廣東話 – *Guangdong wah* – 'Cantonese (language)'
מאמע־לשון – *mame-loshn* – 'Yiddish' (literally 'mother tongue')
The 'sentence' is the final one from Charles Darwin's *On the Origin of Species* and is the only time the word 'evolve', or one of its cognates, appears in the work.
Γένεσις – *genesis* – 'origin'

HAVING JUST BROKEN THE WATER PITCHER: The legendary inventor of Chinese characters was *Cangjie*, court historian to the Yellow Emperor.

On the 'Elephant of Truth' meme, and the evolving menagerie of punning animals invented by China's netizens to bypass censorship, see the *China Digital Times'* 'Grass-Mud Horse Lexicon':
chinadigitaltimes.net/space/Introduction_to_the_Grass-Mud_Horse_Lexicon

THAT FROM A LONG WAY OFF LOOK LIKE FLIES: 'But how, if that fly had a father and mother?' – *Titus Andronicus, 3.2.*

THE COUNTESS OF PEMBROKE'S ARCADIA: Sir Philip Sidney's *Arcadia*, dedicated to his sister Mary, the Countess of Pembroke, remained incomplete on his death in 1586 (aged 31) at the Battle of Zutphen.
veni, veni – 'come, come' – from the letter penned after his mortal wound. This poem is for Gavin Alexander.

ISLANDS: *Ping Chau, Cheung Chau, Lantau, Lamma* – four outlying islands of Hong Kong.
月 – *jyut* – is the simplest Cantonese word for moon, originally a pictograph of its crescent.
Houyi is a mythical Chinese archer. He saved the earth from becoming a scorched desert at the time of the ten Sun Birds by shooting down the nine errant suns with his bow. He was awarded the Elixir of Immortality by the Queen Mother of the West – enough for himself and his wife *Chang'e* – but made the mistake of rushing out to another task, leaving it unsecured.

Acknowledgements

Acknowledgments are due to the editors of the following journals where versions of some of these poems were first published: *Horizon Review, LikeStarlings, Magma, PN Review, Poetry London, Poetry Review, Poetry Wales, Shearsman, Transom, The White Review.*

A number of poems appeared in my pamphlet *A Certain Chinese Encyclopedia* (tall-lighthouse, 2009) and in the following anthologies: *The Best British Poetry 2014* (Salt, 2014), *Ten: The New Wave* (Bloodaxe, 2014), *The Mimic Octopus* (13 pages, 2014), *Dear World & Everyone In It* (Bloodaxe, 2013), *The Best British Poetry 2012* (Salt, 2012), *The Salt Book of Younger Poets* (Salt, 2011).

'Start with Weather' was originally written as part of an exchange with Kirun Kapur.

I am grateful to the Society of Authors for an Eric Gregory Award, to the Hawthornden Foundation for an International Writers' Fellowship, and to the Master and Fellows of St John's College, Cambridge, for a Harper-Wood Studentship in English Poetry and Literature.

My debts are many, but I owe particular thanks to my editor Parisa Ebrahimi for her scrupulous reading; to Nathalie Teitler, Karen McCarthy Woolf, my mentor Bill Herbert and the *Complete Works* family; to Nia Davies, Jorie Graham, Oli Hazzard, John Kerrigan, Vidyan Ravinthiran and Ahren Warner for their advice and support; to Roddy Lumsden and his Wednesday group for their sage friendship down the years; and above all to my parents and my husband Marc, with love.